FINDING

YOUR

BALANCE

FINDING

YOUR

BALANCE

Guided Exercises for
Cognitive Behavioral Therapy

chartwell
books

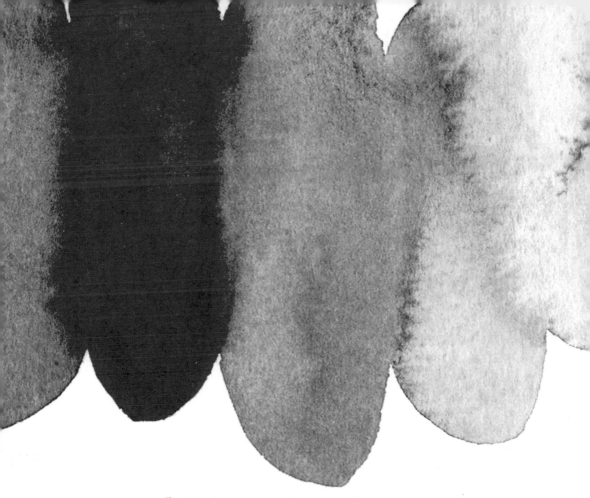

Contents

Introduction

We've all been there many times, stuck in our own heads. The truth is, many of us feel comfortable in that state. It feels safe and familiar. However, if you really pause to notice how much time you spend wrapped up in your thoughts, you'll begin to see just how often you are avoiding the present moment. It is this avoidance of feelings, and escape from the present, that keeps us stuck inside our head. The longer we hang out in there, the worse our stress and anxiety will become. Why, then, do we choose to spend so much time in our head if it's detrimental to our mental wellness? The answer is simple. Sometimes facing our feelings in the present just hurts too much.

Helping people redirect away from their minds and into the moment is the foundation of the work I do in my practice. When I ask patients what their goals are for therapy, the most common responses I get are "I want to feel happier" or "I don't want to ever feel anxious." However, these types of goals make their progress more difficult. You're probably asking yourself, "Why would wanting to feel happier be a bad goal? Don't we all just want to be happy?" In a perfect world, yes, we may choose to be happy all the time. The problem is that no one's world is perfect. We will undoubtedly have a wide range of experiences and emotions throughout our lives.

Having mood-based goals sets us up for failure. Why? Because moods are fluid. Trying to have a permanent mood of any kind is impossible.

Think of happiness as a target you're trying to hit, but one that's constantly moving. You can only push away or avoid painful thoughts and feelings for so long. After a while, trying to hit the bullseye would become frustrating. You would likely start to feel defeated, angry, or worried. Furthermore, this frustration might lead to you to think you are incapable of being happy no matter what you do, creating feelings of hopelessness, helplessness, and a sense of being out of control. It puts you at a much higher risk for anxiety disorders, depression, and an overall decline in mental well-being.

Part of the human experience is feeling all our feelings (yes, even the bad ones). And despite popular opinion, it's okay to not be okay. We can't control what emotions or thoughts come up for us in any given moment. What we can control, however, is how we choose to respond to our emotions, to our thoughts, and to other people.

What Is Anxiety?

"I'm so anxious!" We've all said and heard this phrase countless times. But are we anxious, or stressed? It's important to understand the difference between these two concepts. Stress is a normal response to changes in our everyday lives. Work, family, finances, and relationships all contribute to the stress we feel on a daily basis. The less control we feel over a particular situation, the more likely we are to feel stress.

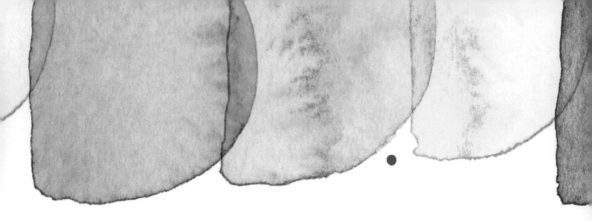

Our bodies are well equipped to deal with stressful events. We have a built-in response system known as "fight or flight." Stress triggers our fight-or-flight mode, which prepares our bodies to effectively manage the situation. And while these physical symptoms may feel bad (e.g., racing heart, shortness of breath, sweating), they are in no way dangerous. In fact, they are extremely beneficial. They inform us about our surroundings and help to keep us safe. However, prolonged stress responses that are left untreated can have a major impact on our bodies over time. Heart disease, chronic pain, insomnia, and a weakened immune system are all chronic effects of long-term stress.

So, if that's stress, then what exactly is anxiety? Anxiety can be characterized by intense feelings of nervousness, extreme worry, intrusive thoughts, and physical symptoms such as dizziness, shakiness, sweating, or increased heart rate. People will often avoid situations that bring about these feelings. At high levels, though, this avoidance can significantly interfere with one's day-to-day functioning. It is important for us to remember that anxiety is a naturally occurring human emotion. For this reason, there's no way to avoid it completely. In fact, it's necessary for our survival and protection. It's what makes us think to look both ways before crossing the street; it's what tells us to run fast if we are being chased by a robber. In moderate amounts, anxiety motivates us to achieve our goals. It pushes us to do well in school, in sports, and at work.

If anxiety can be beneficial, then why does it feel so bad? To start, human beings are wired for survival and contentment, not a permanent state of happiness. Yet, as a society, we have this notion that we must always strive for perfect happiness. So, when we feel anything other than happy, we interpret the feeling as bad and something to get rid of immediately. What happens, though, when our not so happy emotion is the proper emotional response to a situation? For example, if you lost your job, it would be an extremely appropriate response to be sad. But because we are so focused on achieving this goal of happiness, we try hard to avoid any emotion that contradicts it. This is why phrases such as "It could be worse" or "Positive vibes only" can be so invalidating; it's something known as "toxic positivity." Toxic positivity is the idea that we should always be happy, regardless of the situation; that feeling appropriately sad or anxious is somehow bad. However, trying to avoid uncomfortable feelings creates a more intense version of the emotions we are trying so hard to squash.

So, some anxiety is normal, and it can be counterproductive to try to get rid of it entirely. But when anxiety becomes constant and consists of irrational worry that won't turn off, when it begins to cause significant problems in your life (e.g., avoiding people, places, and things that pose no real danger), that's when it may really require attention. If you've been feeling this way, you may have a clinical anxiety disorder.

Anxiety is the most common mental health diagnosis in the United States, affecting approximately forty million adults annually, almost 18 percent of the population. And while anxiety disorders are very treatable, only about 35 percent of people suffering from clinical anxiety receive any type of treatment. Clinical anxiety can present itself in a variety of ways, including social anxiety disorder (SAD), obsessive compulsive disorder (OCD), generalized anxiety disorder (GAD), and panic disorder.

Whether or not your experience of anxiety reaches the level of a clinical anxiety disorder, this workbook can help. It will teach you various techniques to help you sit with your anxiety and stress rather than trying to get rid of them. In addition, it will offer strategies to help you manage day-to-day stress. Just learning how to better manage this everyday stress can help you remain present-focused longer, increase productivity, and lead to an overall improvement in relationships and well-being. Better daily stress management also puts you at a lower risk of developing a clinical anxiety or mood disorder.

To understand our anxiety, we need to break it down into four fundamental components: our emotions, our body, our thoughts, and our behaviors. Our emotions consist of all the feelings that come up for us in any given situation, such as fear, worry, guilt, or sadness. Our body represents the actual physical sensations we experience when we are

anxious (e.g., a racing heartbeat, shallow breathing, upset stomach, and a headache). It also includes physiological changes, such as increases in a stress hormone called cortisol. The third component of anxiety is our thought process, better known as "cognition." This includes the thoughts we have about ourselves, others, and our relationship to the outside world. Some examples of anxious thought processes include "Everyone will laugh at me," "What if my headache isn't just a headache?," or "What if no one likes my business proposal and it gets rejected?" Lastly, we have our behaviors, or what we actually do in response to our anxiety. These behaviors can include anything from eating too much to social isolation. For example, you decide to stay home alone rather than attend a friend's birthday party because you're too anxious to go. Or you have a work presentation in the morning and public speaking makes you horrifically anxious. You wake up the next day, call in sick, and ask your assistant to do the presentation on your behalf.

Being able to break down anxiety into individual parts makes it not only easier to identify but also to treat. It informs us of our triggers (a negative thought, racing heart, or cancelling plans) so that we know what to specifically target. It also allows us to view our anxiety more objectively. By identifying what we are thinking and feeling, we create space between us and our symptoms.

The Role of Avoidance in Anxiety

People naturally function better when they behave in ways consistent with their values. When our behaviors are not in line with our values, our risk of stress, anxiety, and even depression increases. Why then would we purposely behave in direct opposition to the things we value most? Avoidance. We want to avoid our bad emotions and negative thinking. We only want to be in a happy state, so we struggle furiously against anything that threatens it and do whatever we can to not feel bad. Yet in our effort to get rid of that internal ickiness, we make it worse.

For example, let's say you value being a responsible employee. It would make perfect sense that behaviors such as meeting deadlines, being on time, and working hard would all increase your self-esteem, confidence, and performance. Your behaviors are moving you toward your identified value of being a good employee. What if, however, work has really been stressing you out lately? To avoid your work stress, you start calling out, missing meetings, and working less hard because it's just too overwhelming. But this behavior has now resulted in a poor performance review and a lost promotion. While your efforts to get rid of your work stress may have initially provided temporary relief, they ultimately took you further away from what is most important to you.

By avoiding what feels bad, we continue to create more of what we don't want. We also internalize the message that we are incapable of handling difficult emotions. Take drinking alcohol as another example. Many people find socializing in large groups to be extremely anxiety provoking. They fear judgment by others, may feel stupid when in conversations, or sense that they just don't fit in. The unwillingness to sit with those uncomfortable thoughts and feelings while mingling at a party is a big reason why people drink alcohol in these settings. Alcohol temporarily mutes their anxiety. While this suppression might help at first, the relief is short-lived, and the person's belief that they need alcohol to be social is reinforced. It becomes a vicious cycle.

We frequently see this unwillingness to tolerate discomfort in people with perfectionist tendencies. Those who identify as perfectionists have an intense fear of failure. The anxiety they experience when faced with a performance task can be debilitating. To avoid this pain, they procrastinate. They may focus so intently on the tiny details that they lose sight of the larger task and either don't complete it or complete it late. Or they simply never start at all. Both behaviors initially reduce anxiety, but this is only an illusion. By procrastinating and not finishing,

they believe that they are lessening their anxiety. You can't fail if you never finish. But, by procrastinating, they fail anyway, thereby confirming their initial fear. Chances are, those with perfectionist tendencies value being a good student or employee. Yet their behavior (i.e., procrastination) takes them further away from this value, making their anxiety even worse.

So, if it's unhealthy to avoid your anxious thoughts and feelings, then what do you do? You sit with them. You tolerate them. You observe, without judgment, whatever comes up for you in the moment, and then let it pass. You feel the uncomfortable feelings, have the worrisome thoughts, and at the same exact time, move toward what is making you anxious. In other words, feel bad, and do it anyway. It provides you the opportunity to see that nothing bad happens, an experience that you otherwise would have deprived yourself of. By changing or stopping behaviors that are unhealthy, avoidant, or no longer work for us, we decrease our risk for anxiety, relationship difficulties, and mood disorders.

How to Use This Workbook

Unlike traditional self-help books, this anxiety-management workbook offers you uniquely concrete and practical exercises that are rooted in evidence-based treatments, such as acceptance and commitment therapy and mindfulness-based cognitive therapy. Exercises are grouped into three chapters, each of which focuses on a core concept of anxiety management. This workbook will teach you alternative ways to perceive your anxiety, such as how to notice a thought rather than trying to stop yourself from thinking it. You will learn ways to tolerate your anxious feelings rather than avoid them, and how to pay closer attention to your body and recognize the physical sensations of anxiety.

Exercises are specifically designed to be user-friendly, manageable, and easily applied. When people understand why and how a strategy works, they're more likely to apply it to their everyday lives. Be sure to pick exercises that really resonate with you. There is no right or wrong approach to using this workbook. All the strategies are designed to be used at any time and in no particular order.

CHAPTER

YOU ARE NOT YOUR ANXIOUS THOUGHTS

In this chapter, you will find tools and techniques to help you pay attention to your thoughts, allow them to simply exist, then let them pass rather than battling with them. Numerous strategies, such as metaphors and defusion exercises, will teach you how to become objective in your thinking rather than getting entangled with your thoughts and stuck in your head.

A Thought
is Just a Thought

While it may feel as if our anxious thoughts are hard truths, they aren't. In fact, they are just thought bubbles and nothing more. When someone has anxiety, their thoughts become worrisome, irrational, and sometimes ruminative—they just can't shut them off. They start to believe their negative self-statements and inaccurate perceptions of themselves and others. It makes sense that we often try to suppress, ignore, or forget these thoughts. They make us feel bad and uncomfortable! But as discussed earlier, deliberately trying to stop anxious thoughts only makes them stay longer and bring their friends around.

Let's say you are about to become a parent. It is your first child, and you have a significant amount of anxiety about it. "What if I'm not a good mom?" "What if other people think I'm a bad mom?" "What if my child doesn't love me?" While these types of thoughts don't make us happy when we experience them, they happen to be extremely common and appropriate worries for new moms. If you try not to think these very normal thoughts, they will become more pervasive and trick you into believing them.

So, why does this happen? Why can't we get rid of thoughts we don't want to have? You may have heard the saying "That which you water,

grows." The things we choose to direct our energy toward become more powerful. Just like watering a plant to make it grow, the more effort we invest trying to ignore our worry, the bigger it becomes.

Think about what's involved in telling ourselves not to think about something. In order to tell ourselves not to think a thought, we must actually have the thought itself. For example, when you tell yourself not to think about "the blue car," you have to actually say the words "blue car." Basically, by telling yourself not to think something, you ensure that you will think about it. So, how do you stop a thought? By not trying to stop it.

This section includes exercises that will teach you to simply notice your thoughts without judgment, sit with them, then let them pass on their own rather than struggling to get rid of them. These techniques, known as "defusion strategies," help to separate us from our anxious thoughts. They offer ways to regard our thoughts objectively, giving us the ability to look at them instead of being tangled up inside them.

Worry·Art

This exercise teaches you how to separate from your anxious thoughts by using your five senses.

For sixty seconds, do nothing but purposely think about all your worry and anxiety. Pay close attention to the feelings, thoughts, and bodily sensations that come up for you.

When you are finished, record your responses to the following questions:

1.	IF YOUR ANXIETY HAD A HUMAN NAME, WHAT WOULD IT BE?
2.	WHAT COLOR IS YOUR ANXIETY?
3.	IF YOUR ANXIETY HAD A SHAPE, WHAT WOULD IT BE?
4.	WHAT IS THE SIZE OF YOUR ANXIETY?
5.	WHAT DOES YOUR ANXIETY SMELL LIKE?

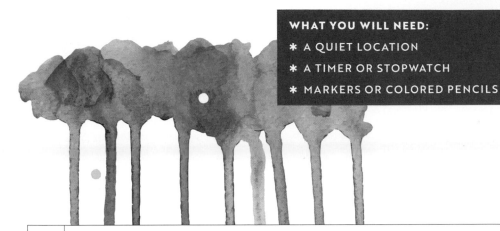

6.	WHAT DOES YOUR ANXIETY WEIGH?

7.	WHAT DOES YOUR ANXIETY FEEL LIKE WHEN YOU TOUCH IT?

8.	WHAT NOISE DOES YOUR ANXIETY MAKE?

NEXT, DRAW A PICTURE OF YOUR WORRY IN THE SPACE PROVIDED:

CHAPTER ONE

Using all the characteristics you imagined for your worry, write out five sentences that can be used to actively separate you from your worry in the moment, something to remind yourself that your worry is not you. For example:

"There goes Marvin again... that green, slimy little oval."

"I hear Marvin's piercing screech again."

"I'm starting to smell Marvin's rotten food stench."

1. _____

2. _____

3.

4.

5.

Word Reframing

Using the word "but" makes your progress seem irrelevant because you still get anxious at times. This then contributes to your existing negative thought pattern.

Using the word "and," however, highlights your progress and suggests you can be both things at the same time: progressing and anxious. This contradicts your negative self-statement, making room for a much healthier one.

Negative self-talk and all-or-nothing thinking are common in anxiety.

The words we use play a critical role in the development and maintenance of our anxiety. Sometimes just the smallest, most subtle shift in the words we use can have a profound impact on our mood.

But vs. And

❖ I know I am making progress in therapy, but I still get anxious.

❖ I know I am making progress in therapy, and I still get anxious.

WHAT DO YOU NOTICE ABOUT THE DIFFERENCE BETWEEN THESE TWO STATEMENTS?

It's a Given

❖ I just sounded so stupid when I ordered my dinner. My date won't want to see me again.

❖ I am having the thought that I just sounded so stupid when I ordered my dinner, and my date won't want to see me again.

WHAT DO YOU NOTICE ABOUT THE DIFFERENCE BETWEEN THESE TWO STATEMENTS?

_____

_____

_____

_____

_____

_____

_____

_____

_____

_____

_____

_____

_____

The first statement presents as a given.

The second statement is simply a thought, not a fact. It puts space between you and your thought. You can look at your thought, rather than being stuck In It.

1. _____
_____
_____
_____
_____
2. _____
_____
_____
_____

Think of a self-statement you may have said or thought recently. Using one of the reframing techniques above, write out the two versions of your self-statement.

WHAT DO YOU NOTICE?

_____
_____
_____
_____
_____

Throughout your day, try to become more aware of the words you choose. When you catch yourself using negative self-statements, substitute a different word and observe any differences.

Write down a few of the substitutions you tried. Does making these kinds of word substitutions change the meaning of what you said? How so?

StickyNote Project

1. First, pick your favorite color for your imaginary sticky notes.

2. Now, imagine a message board located right next to your head.

3. For one minute, just sit and be present. Notice whatever thoughts come up for you during that time.

4. Whenever a thought arises, which could be the same one over and over, mentally write it on a sticky note and stick it to the imaginary message board.

5. Repeat this exercise three times. Once completed, answer the following questions:

This exercise will teach you how to notice your thoughts and let them pass, while acknowledging that they are still very much present.

1.	WHAT DID YOU OBSERVE HAPPENING?

2.	ARE THE THOUGHTS ACTUALLY GONE?

3.	DO THEY FEEL LESS OVERWHELMING?

The separation between you and your thoughts makes them less real and less intrusive and takes you out of your head, thereby keeping you more focused on the present.

Netflix & Worry

Here, you'll practice a way to carry your thoughts differently.

For one minute, simply sit and worry. Worry about everything you need to get done this week, a deadline you have, an argument with a friend, or just anything that has been bothering you. After the minute is up, take a five-minute break to do something entirely unrelated.

Now, for another minute, think about all your worries again. This time, however, imagine you are watching your anxious thoughts projected onto a TV screen as if they are the closing credits.

1.	WHAT DID YOU OBSERVE?

WHAT YOU WILL NEED:
* A QUIET LOCATION
* A TIMER OR STOPWATCH

2.	OF THE TWO SCENARIOS, WHICH ONE FELT LIKE MORE OF AN INTERNAL STRUGGLE? WHY?

3.	WHICH ONE WAS EASIER FOR YOU AND WHY?

Lost Luggage

Imagine standing at the baggage carousel at the airport waiting for your luggage. The carousel turns on, and the bags start coming out. Just like our thoughts, the bags go around and around. On the next page, write down five of the worrisome thoughts that keep coming around for you.

This strategy focuses on how to manage ruminative thinking. Ruminative thinking is when certain thoughts play over and over again in our minds no matter how hard we try to stop them. In fact, the more we try to stop them, the faster the thoughts will loop. Imagine playing the same song on repeat with a broken stop button. Every time you attempt to stop the music, it just makes the same song play faster and faster. This is how ruminative thinking works.

1. _____
_____
_____

2. _____
_____
_____

3. _____
_____
_____

4. _____
_____
_____

5. _____
_____
_____

Even if you pick up a bag, a new one pops right out. If you keep picking up every bag that comes out, you will become exhausted, overwhelmed, and buried in luggage . . . with more still coming out. What is the best thing to do? Simply watch the bags go around. Don't pick them up. Our thoughts work in much the same way as the luggage on the carousel. When we grab on to a thought by worrying about it, ruminating, or struggling to push it away, we become mentally and physically exhausted. Like holding on to your bags, holding on to anxious thoughts weighs us down. It takes us out of the present and prevents us from focusing on the things we enjoy most in life.

Now, imagine that each of your thoughts is a piece of luggage on the carousel. Any new thoughts you have are immediately added to the carousel.

WHAT DO YOU THINK WOULD HAPPEN IF YOU KEPT PICKING UP EVERY ONE OF YOUR BAGS AS THEY CAME AROUND?

IF THERE IS NO END TO THE NUMBER OF BAGS YOU NEED TO CLAIM ON THE CAROUSEL, WHAT DO YOU THINK IS THE BEST WAY TO HANDLE THIS SITUATION?

Designing Defusion

This exercise will teach you how a strategy known as "cognitive defusion," or "thought defusion," can help you become more objective about the thoughts running around in your mind. Rather than trying to control them by attempting to stop or modify your thinking, you actually let go of this control and simply allow the thoughts to exist. Don't talk to them or engage with them in any way. Just let them be.

COME UP WITH YOUR OWN METAPHOR TO DEMONSTRATE THE CONCEPT OF THOUGHT DEFUSION. CHOOSE A TOPIC OR IDEA THAT YOU ENJOY SO THAT THE METAPHOR RESONATES WITH YOU, MAKING IT MORE ACCESSIBLE IN YOUR DAILY LIFE.

_____

_____

_____

_____

_____

_____

_____

_____

_____

_____

_____

_____

_____

_____

_____

_____

_____

_____

_____

_____

_____

Picture your favorite board game. You are the board, your thoughts the pieces. Just like your thoughts, the pieces move around every which way. What remains consistent at all times, regardless of how the pieces are moving above, is the board. Just as the board exists separate from the pieces and is unchanged by their movements, you are separate from your thoughts. This metaphor is a great example of how defusion works.

Come up with a few examples of other statements you can use to reword your anxious thoughts and create some distance between you and them.

1.

2.

3.

4.

5.

In addition to metaphors, our language also plays a very important role in thought defusion. The words we use to speak to ourselves when we worry, feel stressed, or are just going about our day-to-day lives influence our ability to be objective in our thinking.

When a recurring worry comes up, try saying something simple such as "There it is again!" Notice this statement doesn't engage with the worry or try to push it away. It simply allows the worry to exist outside of you. There is no effort to control anything and subsequently no struggle.

Another helpful statement is "My anxiety is telling me . . ." This open-ended statement allows you to acknowledge the content of your anxious thought and gives the impression that you are a separate entity from your anxiety. Instead of saying to yourself, "I'll never pass that test," you'd say, "My anxiety is telling me I'll never pass that test." Rephrasing your worry in this way gives you room to look at your worry rather struggling against it.

WAS IT EASY FOR YOU TO COME UP WITH YOUR OWN EXAMPLES?

_____

_____

_____

_____

_____

WHAT, IF ANYTHING, DID YOU FIND DIFFICULT ABOUT THIS NEW WAY OF
LOOKING AT YOUR THOUGHTS?

_____

_____

_____

_____

_____

_____

THINK OF A FEW COMMON WORRIES OR ANXIOUS THOUGHTS THAT YOU
FREQUENTLY EXPERIENCE AND RECORD THEM BELOW.

_____

_____

_____

_____

_____

_____

USING ONE OF YOUR METAPHORS OR DEFUSION STATEMENTS, REPHRASE THE
FREQUENTLY OCCURRING THOUGHTS YOU PROVIDED ABOVE.

COMPARE THE NEW STATEMENTS TO THE ORIGINAL THOUGHTS.
WHAT DO YOU NOTICE?

Just Passing

Take a moment to imagine yourself living through this experience with the train. Notice any feelings, thoughts, or sensations that come up for you during the train analogy, particularly once you realize that you are unable to get rid of the train, but instead must let it pass on its own.

Imagine the following scene: You are having dinner with your family, and just as the appetizers are being served, a loud train starts passing by the back of your house. It is so loud, so massive, that your table starts to shake. You can no longer hear the dinner conversation. You can't think; you can't concentrate; you can't do anything else but focus on the deafening noise.

If you had superhero strength, you might try to stop the train, but this wouldn't actually solve your problem. Rather, it would prolong the noise at its loudest point, since the train would be stopped directly outside your house. Similarly, trying to stop an uncomfortable thought will only make it louder and more pervasive. The best solution in this case is to do nothing and simply let the train, and the thought, pass through like an unwanted guest.

Through

WHAT WAS THE THOUGHT OR EXPERIENCE?

_____
_____
_____
_____
_____
_____
_____
_____
_____
_____
_____
_____
_____
_____
_____
_____
_____
_____

In the next few days, notice any moments you may have that feel similar to this, where you have an anxious thought or uncomfortable experience. Instead of trying to stop the thought or experience, simply let it pass or run its course. Record how this went by answering these questions.

DID IT MAKE YOU ANXIOUS? DID YOU FEEL A LOSS OF CONTROL? A SENSE OF
HOPELESSNESS? MAYBE EVEN SOME ANGER?

HOW DID IT FEEL TO LET IT PASS WITHOUT TRYING TO STOP IT?

The Purple Flower

This exercise, adapted from one by Steven Hayes, PhD, is an extremely effective strategy for demonstrating how forcing yourself to not think about something makes you focus on it harder.

❖ **Scenario A:**

For one minute, do nothing but think about a purple flower. What does it smell like? What does it look like? What shade of purple is it? What does it feel like? Where are you? Are you in a garden, in a flower shop, in a field? How many other purple flowers are there?

❖ **Scenario B:**

Repeat the exercise. But this time, do not think about a purple flower. If a purple flower comes into your mind at any point during this exercise, make sure you stop thinking about it immediately, push it away, and think about something else. You can even provide yourself prompts such as "Whatever you do, don't think about the purple flower."

When you are done, record your answers to the questions on the following pages.

1.	WHICH SCENARIO, A OR B, FELT LIKE MORE OF A STRUGGLE?

2.	WHICH SCENARIO, A OR B, WAS MORE INTENSE?

3.	WHICH SCENARIO, A OR B, MADE YOU MORE UNCOMFORTABLE?

Since you thought about the purple flower in both scenarios anyway, ask yourself this: Would you rather think about the purple flower and be stressed, anxious, and exhausted? Or would you rather think about the purple flower and feel at ease and stay present-focused?

When we tell ourselves not to think about the purple flower, we must actually say the words purple flower in our head. To not think about a thought, we must think it anyway.

Your Own Worst Enemy

The way we speak to, and about, ourselves inside our own head can result in a significant amount of anxiety. It's almost as if we have an evil villain with a megaphone who rents space deep within our minds. And when he feels threatened, he picks up his megaphone and shouts judgmental and overly critical statements to us about our abilities and self-worth.

This exercise will help you to identify some of your fault-finding self-statements and figure out what to do with them.

1. _____

_____

_____

_____

2. _____

_____

_____

_____

_____

3. _____

_____

_____

_____

4. _____

_____

_____

_____

5. _____

_____

_____

_____

_____

Examples of negative self-statements include "I'm not good enough to get promoted," "I need to be perfect or I'm nothing," and "People think I'm dumb."

What are some of your overly critical self-statements?

WHEN DO THEY COME UP FOR YOU? WHAT TRIGGERS THEM?

WHAT DO YOU NOTICE?

Instead of trying to suppress them or ignore them, pick one of your defusion statements (page 44) to create some distance between you and the thoughts.

Down the Rabbit Hole

1. Find a comfortable position, and for one minute, sit quietly and just observe the space around you.

2. Notice how your back feels against the chair, how your feet feel on the floor, the sound of the low humming of the refrigerator in the other room, the smell of the smoke from the candle you just blew out, the taste of mint in your mouth from just brushing your teeth . . .

3. Record your observations. How difficult was this for you? What was most difficult about it? Did thoughts come into your mind and take you out of the present and down the rabbit hole?

This strategy can help you identify how frequently you fall into the trap of negative thinking and find a way to pull yourself back out.

_____

_____

_____

_____

_____

_____

_____

_____

_____

Repeat this same exercise two more times with a minute break in between. As best you can, try to track the number of times you go down the rabbit hole of your thoughts—write the number in the space below. The act of tracking will also help as an anchor point to bring you back into the present moment.

RABBIT HOLE TRACKING:

SECOND ATTEMPT:	THIRD ATTEMPT:

Repeat the exercise one last time. But now, when you catch yourself drifting off in thought, use a defusion statement (page 44) to pull you out. Track, as best you can, how many times you use your defusion statement. Saying something such as "I'm doing it again" not only brings you back to the present moment but also helps to separate you from your thinking.

NUMBER OF TIMES:

Over the course of your week, repeat this exercise twice a day using various defusion statements. Make sure to track your attempts in the space provided below.

	SUNDAY	MONDAY	TUESDAY
1st Attempt			
2nd Attempt			

The goal is to show a gradual decrease in the times you go down the rabbit hole as you become more comfortable staying present, noticing your thoughts, and separating from them.

AFTER A WEEK OF THIS PRACTICE, WHAT DO YOU NOTICE? HAS ANYTHING CHANGED ABOUT YOUR NEGATIVE THINKING?

_____

_____

_____

_____

_____

WEDNESDAY	THURSDAY	FRIDAY	SATURDAY

It's Worry Time!

This exercise demonstrates how worry is an avoidant strategy we use to disconnect from uncomfortable feelings. As long as we are in our head worrying, we are not sitting in the present with our anxious feelings. Worry is simply an illusion of control. It tricks us into thinking we are problem solving, when, really, we are just sitting in our heads, on a couch, having done absolutely nothing for twenty minutes. While it appears to be an effective form of problem-solving at first, it is an inefficient and ineffective strategy that ultimately worsens anxiety as well as sleep, concentration, and attention.

AFTER A WEEK OF THIS PRACTICE, WHAT DO YOU NOTICE? HAS ANYTHING CHANGED ABOUT YOUR NEGATIVE THINKING?

_____
_____
_____
_____
_____
_____
_____
_____
_____
_____
_____
_____
_____

Anytime you catch yourself worrying throughout the day, use your defusion strategies from the prior exercises to separate from your worries. Place your worries on a mental bookshelf for later reading. This will also help you to remain more present-focused during your day.

CHAPTER ONE

65

Next, choose a specific time in your day to be your two-minute designated worry time (try to make it approximately the same time every day for consistency). It is helpful to block off your worry time in your calendar or smartphone as a daily activity. During worry time, you will return to your mental bookshelf and read all the books you placed there throughout your day.

WHAT DID YOU NOTICE DURING YOUR WORRY TIME?

_____

_____

_____

_____

_____

_____

_____

_____

_____

_____

_____

_____

_____

_____

_____

_____

_____

_____

_____

_____

It is likely that you forgot several of your worries from the day, many of the ones you did remember never came to fruition, and those that did no longer seem as significant.

CHAPTER

2.

BEING WITH
YOUR BODY

The exercises in this chapter teach you ways to pay attention to the physical sensations in your body. Strategies include mindfulness and grounding techniques to help you remain in the present moment while also sitting with the physical discomfort that comes up during times of stress and anxiety.

Sitting with the Scary Stuff

We have all felt it: that sudden pang of anxiety in your stomach, the rush of warm adrenaline through your chest, the numbing tingle of panic in your fingertips. We do everything in our power to avoid those dreaded sensations, yet they seem to happen anyway. If we try so hard not to have these sensations, why then do they seem to attack us with a vengeance? The answer, yet again, is avoidance. As with our thoughts, when we avoid our internal physical discomfort, we make those sensations more intense, longer lasting, and more frequent.

While these sensations can be extremely uncomfortable, even downright scary at times, they are not harmful. The racing heart, shortness of breath, and dizziness of a panic attack are not fatal. You will not pass out; you will not die. The numbness and tingling in your extremities and face brought on by intense panic are not the result of a stroke or seizure. In fact, what you are experiencing is your body's way of alerting you to apparent danger. The good news is that your body is doing what it should be doing, even though no real danger exists. So why does this happen?

These physical sensations are adaptive responses. They alert us to danger and provide us with information about our environment to keep us safe. When our brain senses danger is near, it sends a message down into our body to prep for fight-or-flight mode. For example, if a lion were chasing us down the street, our brain would communicate to our heart to beat faster for increased blood flow and energy and to our lungs to take shorter and quicker breaths. It would cause our muscles to tense as a way to prepare us for action and our pupils to dilate to help us see our surroundings better.

In the normal stress response, hormones are released to prompt our body to respond to the threat. Adrenaline is responsible for elevating our heart rate and blood pressure and filling us up with the energy we need to combat the danger that awaits us. Another stress hormone known as cortisol releases excess sugar, or glucose, into our blood. During fight-or-flight mode, cortisol suppresses several systems in our body to limit

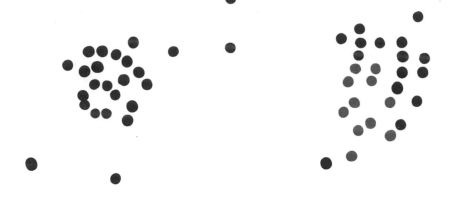

any nonessential bodily functions that could impair our ability to protect ourselves from danger.

The issue arises, however, when these same physical sensations suddenly occur when there is no real threat or danger present. Rather, these feelings are falsely triggered in response to a perceived threat or danger. This is very common in panic attacks, specific phobias, and in social anxiety disorder. When stress and anxiety are left untreated for long periods of time, our bodies remain in a chronic state of fight or flight, which has a significant impact not only on our mental well-being but also on our body. The impact of long-term chronic stress and anxiety, including prolonged exposure to stress hormones, can lead to an overall weakened immune system, chronic pain, migraines, chronic fatigue, and higher risks for many other diseases, such as heart disease, diabetes, and even cancer.

Again, it is important to remember that these physical sensations are not harmful. And while they may feel uncomfortable, they are an indicator that your body is doing exactly what it should be doing. It's adapting to keep you safe, preparing you to fight or run. But when there is no

real danger, we don't need to prepare for battle. All this excess energy has nowhere to go! And it would seem reasonable that we would want to do anything we could to avoid and push away these sensations. Yet, just as with our thoughts, avoiding these sensations only makes them worse. They build up in our body, keeping us in a chronic and vicious loop of body dysregulation (e.g., elevated heart rate and blood pressure). We often see avoidance of these bad feelings in the context of substance abuse or other addictions, isolation, worry, depression, panic, and PTSD. But these numbing efforts are ineffective solutions that create even more of the bad feelings you are trying to get rid of.

The most effective way to manage these feelings is to allow yourself to have them, fully, in the moment. Rather than trying to escape, avoid, or ignore these sensations, you need to sit with them; do absolutely nothing except have them until they pass . . . because they will. Sitting with the scary stuff not only improves nervous-system dysregulation but also results in healthier behaviors and choices.

Balloon Breathing

As we get older, the way in which we breathe tends to change. We experience more life stressors and triggers, and as a result our bodies can become more and more dysregulated. The truth is, most people breathe incorrectly! We tend to do what's called "shoulder-shrug breathing."

When we take a breath in, our chest and shoulders lift upward; when we exhale, our shoulders and chest fall back down. While it may seem like a quicker way to get a breath, this way of breathing drastically limits the amount of air we can take into our lungs. Yet, these short shoulder-shrug breaths do serve a distinct purpose. In fight-or-flight mode, shorter breaths allow oxygen to get into our lungs in the fastest way possible. They increase our heart rate, make our blood pump faster, and increase the production of the stress hormone cortisol—all vital body responses when we are facing a threat. The problem is that most of us use shoulder-shrug breathing when we are not facing a real threat of danger. This tricks our body into responding as if we were in danger, often putting us at higher risk for anxiety and/or a panic attack.

If you look at babies and animals, you will notice that when they breathe, their stomachs move up and down, not their chests. This is proper breathing technique. When we take a breath in, our stomachs should rise with air; when we exhale, our stomachs should go down. We can get deeper, slower, more controlled breaths. Our chest and shoulders, when engaged in proper breathing technique, shouldn't really move at all!

WHAT YOU WILL NEED:
* A QUIET LOCATION
* A MIRROR THAT ALLOWS YOU TO SEE YOUR BODY FROM THE WAIST UP

WHICH BODY PARTS MOVED THIS TIME FOR YOU? DID YOU NOTICE HOW YOUR BREATHING WAS DEEPER AND SLOWER, ALLOWING FOR CALMER BREATHS?

This "balloon breathing" exercise teaches proper breathing technique to help regulate our bodies and reduce stress and anxiety.

Now, pick your favorite color balloon. Imagine this balloon in your belly. While standing in front of the mirror again:

1. Take a deep breath in for five seconds while visualizing your balloon filling up with air.

2. Hold for five seconds.

3. Exhale to a count of five while visualizing your balloon deflating in your belly.

Try practicing this exercise three times a day while in a relatively relaxed state of mind. Your ability to be mindful of your breath will be significantly better when you are not distracted by stress and worry.

AFTER A WEEK OR SO OF PRACTICING THIS EXERCISE, DO YOU NOTICE ANYTHING DIFFERENT ABOUT YOUR BREATHING OR YOUR RESPONSE IN STRESSFUL SITUATIONS?

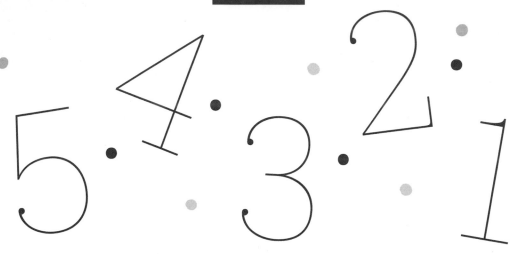

Using your balloon breathing skills from the exercise on page 75, take a few deep breaths in and out. While maintaining appropriate breathing technique, begin to take inventory of your immediate surroundings using your five senses, beginning with your sight.

A common way to help ground ourselves in the present moment is to take deliberate and active steps to bring ourselves out of our worry spirals. One way to do this is by using our five senses to guide us. This technique, originally created by the SOAR program, is an easy way to lift ourselves out of our mind and connect with the physical world around us.

What is so great about this easy strategy is that you can put it into use at any point in your day (e.g., while washing dishes, in a meeting, playing a sport, or giving a presentation), even during times of low stress, to prevent any escalation of worry and anxiety.

5. Notice five things you can see around you. Say them in your mind or out loud. (Don't forget to maintain your balloon breathing.)

4. Notice four things you can touch in your immediate area. Feel the textures and weights of the objects.

3. Notice three things you can hear; notice the differences in tone, volume, and frequency. Again, remember to maintain your balloon breathing!

2. Notice two things you can smell; notice the differences in fragrances, the strengths of each, and so on.

1. Notice one thing you can taste. If you don't have anything directly available to you, you can do something as simple as put the end of a pen in your mouth, taste your own saliva, and so on. It does not need to be an edible object.

At the end of this exercise, always take some additional time to simply sit and conclude with two to three deep balloon breaths.

WHAT DID YOU NOTICE AROUND YOU DURING THIS EXERCISE?

_____

_____

_____

_____

_____

_____

_____

HOW DID YOU FEEL BEFORE YOU BEGAN?

_____

_____

_____

_____

_____

_____

_____

_____

HOW DID YOU FEEL WHEN THE EXERCISE WAS COMPLETE?

_____

_____

_____

_____

_____

_____

_____

_____

_____

_____

_____

_____

_____

_____

_____

_____

_____

_____

Shoulders & Ears

Should Not Be Neighbors

One of the most glossed-over symptoms of everyday stress and anxiety is muscle tension, particularly tension in our neck, shoulders, back, abdomen, head, and even face. Often, we don't realize just how much this muscle tightness impacts our daily functioning. We may think we slept funny or even pinched something while bending down. However, it is very likely that our muscles are already tight from stress. This ongoing tension can result in chronic inflammation and prolonged production of unnecessary stress hormones, and it leaves our bodies susceptible to weakened immune-system functioning and illness. It is important for both our mental and physical health that we remain mindful of where stress is stored in our body so that we can be proactive in targeting it early.

This exercise is an excellent way to increase body awareness and notice how tension directly impacts our muscles. You will develop skills to become more mindful of your body, while paying special attention to tension-prone areas.

WHAT YOU WILL NEED:

* FOUR SMALL PIECES OF TAPE OR A PENCIL WITH AN ERASER
* A FLAT SURFACE TO STAND AGAINST, SUCH AS A WALL OR DOOR

TAKE A STEP BACK FROM THE WALL AND EXAMINE YOUR TWO SETS OF SHOULDER MARKINGS. WHAT DO YOU NOTICE?

_____

_____

_____

_____

_____

_____

_____

_____

_____

_____

_____

_____

_____

_____

_____

_____

_____

1. Stand with your back firmly against a wall or flat surface. Make sure your heels, back, shoulders, and back of head are flush against the wall.

2. Take two pieces of tape or a pencil and mark on the wall exactly where each of your shoulders line up on the wall. If this is too difficult to do on your own, you can have someone mark it for you. Leave these markers up for the duration of the exercise.

3. While standing with your back and shoulders to the wall, engage in either balloon breathing (page 74) or the 5-4-3-2-1 exercise (page 78). When finished, remark your shoulder placement on the wall with tape or pencil. Remember to leave your original markers up there!

HOW DID THE TENSION IN YOUR BODY FEEL BEFORE THIS EXERCISE,
AND HOW DOES IT FEEL AFTER?

_____

_____

_____

_____

_____

_____

_____

_____

_____

_____

_____

_____

_____

_____

_____

_____

_____

_____

_____

_____

_____

_____

_____

_____

_____

_____

_____

_____

_____

_____

_____

_____

_____

Try this exercise daily, particularly after times that you identify as high stress. Becoming mindful of your body's reaction to stress is a great way to help reduce tension throughout your day. Even just the slightest reduction in muscle tenseness can help reduce stress hormones.

EXERCISE

Surprise!

Imagine it's your birthday. You and your significant other walk into a restaurant to celebrate the special day. The hostess escorts you to a table in the back room, and as you walk in, twenty of your closest family members and friends jump out and yell "Surprise!"

Often when we are stressed, our thoughts, feelings, behaviors, and physical self can become jumbled into one big ball of anxiety. One helpful way to tease all this apart is to pay close attention to the physical sensations that arise in your body. Shortness of breath, rapid heartbeat, dizziness, sweating, and shakiness are common indicators of stress or anxiety.

While these symptoms may feel bad, even scary at times, they are in no way dangerous. They are naturally occurring sensations that we label as scary, bad, or anxious. The label we place on them is what impacts our perception and influences the choices we make. This exercise helps demonstrate how the words we use to interpret our bodily sensations contribute to our anxiety.

WRITE DOWN FIVE PHYSICAL SENSATIONS YOU WOULD LIKELY EXPERIENCE IN THIS SITUATION. REMEMBER, PHYSICAL SENSATIONS ARE THINGS YOU FEEL IN YOUR BODY (E.G., SHAKINESS), NOT THOUGHTS OR EMOTIONS (E.G., HAPPINESS, SHOCK).

1.

2.

3.

4.

5.

Now, we are going to repeat this same exercise, except this time you are going to imagine yourself at the zoo. You think you hear faint screams in the distance but aren't quite sure. Suddenly, you see a large group of people running toward you, screaming that a lion has gotten loose. You immediately start running for the exit.

WRITE DOWN FIVE PHYSICAL SENSATIONS YOU WOULD LIKELY EXPERIENCE IN THIS SITUATION. AGAIN, PHYSICAL SENSATIONS ARE THINGS YOU FEEL IN YOUR BODY, NOT THOUGHTS OR EMOTIONS (E.G., FEAR).

1.

2.

3.

4.

5.

WHAT DO YOU NOTICE WHEN COMPARING YOUR ANSWERS TO BOTH SCENARIOS?

You may have noticed a lot of similarities between your physical responses in both scenarios. This is because the bodily sensations we experience are simply that, sensations. They are neither good nor bad. They are just feelings we notice occurring in our bodies. It is the label we choose to attach to them (e.g., exciting, scary, shocking) that gives them a specific meaning.

Next time these feelings arise, pause and ask yourself, "Am I safe?" If the answer is yes, remind yourself that you are experiencing harmless and temporary physical responses, no different than walking into a surprise party! They are the same sensations.

When you notice yourself feeling fear in everyday life, what are your physical responses?

How does recognizing and accepting these physical responses change the way you feel in the moment?

_____

_____

_____

_____

_____

_____

_____

_____

_____

Become a Grounding • Guru •

The objective is to pay attention in the present moment, without judgment, and notice when your thoughts have carried you away. The goal isn't to never drift away, but instead to notice that you have drifted and bring yourself back to the present task at hand.

We live in such a fast-paced society that we rarely notice the details around us. We are constantly on our phones, online, and in our heads. We are rarely present. Using the prompts below, practice just simply being grounded in the moment during daily basic tasks (e.g., brushing your teeth, folding your laundry).

The Shower:

✤ Feel the water on your skin.
   Is it hot? Cold?

✤ Notice how your skin feels when you
   use soap. Soft? Slippery?

✤ Notice the soap suds. How do they feel?
   Smell? Look?

✤ Notice how your scalp feels while
   washing your hair, how the
   shampoo feels on your head.

✤ Describe the patterns made by the
   water droplets on the shower tile,
   curtain, or door.

Cooking:

✤ Feel the water on your hands while
   washing produce.

✤ Notice the smell of the spices.

✤ Notice the textures of the foods
   in your hands.

✤ Pay attention to the colors.

✤ Notice the heat of the pan or oven.

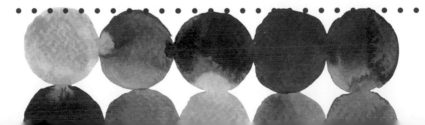

WHAT DO YOU NOTICE HAPPENS DURING THESE GROUNDING TASKS?

DID THESE TECHNIQUES CHANGE YOUR EXPERIENCE OF THE SITUATION?

IF YES, HOW SO?

WHAT DID YOU FIND MOST DIFFICULT?

HOW WAS IT MOST HELPFUL?

LIST THREE ADDITIONAL DAILY ACTIVITIES TO PRACTICE WITH. TRY PRACTICING ONE GROUNDING EXERCISE A WEEK AND TAKE SOME NOTES BELOW ABOUT HOW IT IMPACTS BOTH YOUR MOOD AND ENGAGEMENT.

1.

2.

3.

THESE ARE A FEW OF MY
Favorite Things

Pick three general categories (e.g., movies, music, vegetables) and list them below. For each category, list your top three favorites (e.g., beets, carrots, peas).

This grounding technique uses categorization strategies to remove you from the chaos of your mind and bring you into the present moment.

By focusing on a cognitive task such as listing items by category, you are forced to direct, and sustain, your attention to the present task.

1.
   A
   B
   C

2.
   A
   B
   C

3.
   A
   B
   C

After completing this mental exercise, answer the questions On the following pages:

WHAT DID YOU NOTICE ABOUT YOUR THOUGHTS AND FEELINGS WHILE ENGAGED IN THIS EXERCISE?

WHAT DID YOU FIND MOST DIFFICULT ABOUT THIS EXERCISE?

_____
_____
_____
_____
_____
_____
_____
_____
_____

WHAT DID YOU FIND HELPFUL?

_____
_____
_____
_____
_____
_____
_____
_____
_____

WHERE/WHEN IN YOUR DAY-TO-DAY LIFE DO YOU THINK A STRATEGY SUCH AS THIS WOULD BE MOST HELPFUL TO YOU?

Scan the System

Often, we don't recognize how and where in our bodies we hold stress. We tend to not even notice until we wake up one morning with a sore neck or a migraine. This exercise will teach you how to gain awareness of all your body parts by mentally scanning yourself from top to bottom. Body scanning helps you notice any pain, muscle tension, or general discomfort throughout your body. It also improves mental and physical wellness by reducing the stress hormones in your body.

The goal of scanning is not to get rid of the discomfort but rather to notice where in your body you are carrying it so that you can manage it in a more effective way. This technique can be used when you are feeling anxious or can be implemented as part of your daily wellness routine.

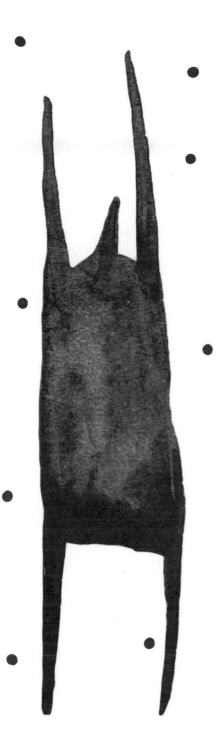

First, shade in the areas on the figure where you would say you typically carry your stress and tension.

1. Get comfy. Lie down or sit in a comfortable chair.

2. Engage in balloon breathing (page 74) for a few moments to help you relax and ground yourself in the present moment.

3. Should you notice that your thoughts take you away from your body, gently bring your awareness back to the body part you were observing before you "left."

4. Start by directing your attention to your toes. Wiggle them around, bend them, flex them. Simply notice any sensations or pain that may be present. Should you observe any discomfort, don't ignore it. Instead, acknowledge the sensation and continue with your balloon breathing.

5. Repeat step 4 for each body part, moving upward until you get to the top of your head. Notice any tension or discomfort and where you hold it. Continue to breathe through the scan using your balloon breathing technique. Redirect your thoughts back to the present moment when you've realized they have taken you away.

Remember, the goal isn't to alleviate your muscle tension but rather to make you aware of its presence.

After completing your body scan, shade in the areas on the figure where you felt any pain, tension, or general discomfort.

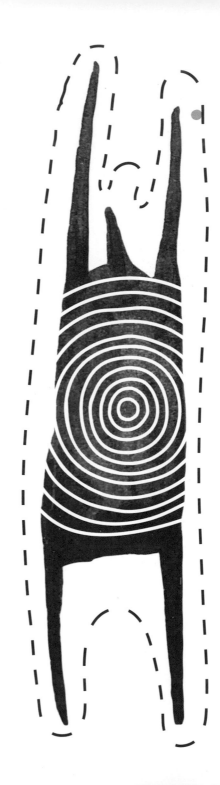

COMPARE YOUR BEFORE AND AFTER BODY MARKINGS. ARE THEY SIMILAR?
DIFFERENT? DO YOU NOTICE ANY PATTERNS?

Continue practicing your scan once a day, noticing any changes in the
location and frequency of your muscle tension and discomfort. Once
you become more familiar with this technique, you can focus on specific
body regions for quick scans.

Muscle (RE)Group

Our bodies are well equipped to manage healthy levels of daily stress. However, when we experience heightened levels of stress and anxiety, our brain thinks we are in danger. This sends our body into fight-or-flight mode, causing our muscles to tighten. Yet, when no real threat is present, this constant muscle tension can lead to chronic pain, illness, and decreased emotional well-being.

By deliberately tensing, then relaxing, each muscle group in a particular order, you can reduce muscle tension and decrease stress and anxiety.

CHAPTER TWO

1. Find a relaxing and comfortable space. You can do this exercise while lying down on a soft surface or sitting in a comfortable chair. Be sure to uncross your arms, legs, and ankles.

2. Begin by taking three balloon breaths (page 74) while allowing your body to fall into a relaxed state.

3. Bring your awareness to your toes. Take a deep balloon breath in and tense and flex your toes for five to ten seconds. Be sure to notice how this tension feels in your body.

4. Take a deep balloon breath out as you immediately release the tension in your toes. This should be a sudden release rather than gradual.

5. Take about fifteen seconds to relax and regroup. Bring your awareness to your body, with specific attention to your toes. How do they feel now compared to when you had them tensed?

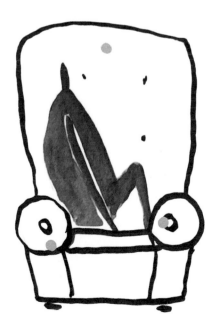

6. Repeat steps 2 to 5 for each of the following muscle groups in this order:

* Feet
* Bottom half of legs
* Thighs
* Buttocks
* Stomach
* Back (lower, middle, shoulder blade area)
* Hands
* Arms (lower and bicep)
* Shoulders
* Neck
* Jaw
* Face
* Lips/smile, nose, eyes
* Forehead

7. Relax for twenty seconds, then tense your entire body and release for ten seconds.

8. Take some time to stretch and breathe. Count backward from ten to slowly bring yourself back to the present moment. Take your time getting up as you may feel a bit lightheaded.

WHAT DID YOU NOTICE WHILE DOING THIS EXERCISE?

_____

_____

_____

_____

_____

_____

_____

HOW DID YOUR BODY FEEL WHILE TENSED COMPARED TO WHILE IN A RELAXED STATE?

_____

_____

_____

_____

_____

_____

_____

_____

_____

Aim to practice this exercise once a day. As you become familiar with this routine, you can shorten it to focus on specific problematic muscle groups.

Time Task Tricks

Being mindful while dealing with the stress of our daily lives can be very difficult. Yet it is the act of being present, despite feeling anxious, that tells our brains we are safe. It confirms that we are not actively facing a real threat, and therefore, our bodies do not need to respond as if we are in danger.

A great way to practice bringing our attention to the present moment is to incorporate mindfulness skills into our day-to-day routines. One method is to focus on a single task, broken down into smaller steps, for a specific amount of time. Not only does this help keep us present by weeding out unnecessary distractions, but it also increases the likelihood that we will complete the task. It creates feelings of accomplishment and an overall reduction in daily stress and worry. Plus, what's better than checking something off our to-do list?

1.

a) _____

b) _____

c) _____

d) _____

e) _____

2.

a) _____

b) _____

c) _____

d) _____

e) _____

3.

a) _____

b) _____

c) _____

d) _____

e) _____

In the space provided, make a daily task list for yourself. Break each task down into three to five subtasks, noting the steps you'll need to complete to finish the task.

CHAPTER TWO

Set your timer for fifteen to twenty minutes. During this time, you are to complete only one of the subtasks. When you find that your attention drifts away from the task, simply bring yourself back to whatever it is that you are doing. Remember, it is normal that our thoughts take us out of the present. The goal is to bring yourself back once you realize you've "left."

4.

a)

b)

c)

d)

e)

5.

a)

b)

c)

d)

e)

6.

a)

b)

c)

d)

e)

ONCE YOU HAVE COMPLETED A SUBTASK, TAKE A MOMENT TO NOTICE YOUR EXPERIENCE. WHAT DID YOU FIND MOST DIFFICULT?

_____

_____

_____

_____

WHAT DID YOU NOTICE ABOUT YOUR ABILITY TO REMAIN FOCUSED ON THE TASK?

_____

_____

_____

_____

_____

WHAT HELPED YOU TO REMAIN PRESENT?

_____

_____

_____

_____

_____

_____

Practicing these single-task exercises even just twice a day can significantly reduce overall stress and anxiety as well as increase productivity.

CHAPTER

3

YOU'VE
GOTTA FEEL IT
TO HEAL IT

Here, we'll focus on strategies that teach you how to sit with, and tolerate, the discomfort of your stress and anxiety. Why would you want to sit with your anxiety? Anxiety and stress become increasingly intense the more you try to not feel them. In fact, the things we do to push away bad feelings are often the very behaviors responsible for making these feelings worse. The exercises that follow will provide you with the skills to be comfortable being uncomfortable, rather than struggling against painful emotions.

You Don't Have to Like It, but You Do Need to Have It

Of course, no one likes to feel anxious. It's consuming and exhausting. However, as mentioned earlier, anxiety is a naturally occurring emotion our bodies use to provide information about our surroundings and keep us safe. Because we need a certain amount of anxiety to survive, it is impossible to fully get rid of it.

So, what do we do with it? We have it. We don't have to like it. We don't have to want it. But we do need to make space for it and feel it. We need to feel all of our anxiety, fully present in the moment, without judgment. Often when people experience stress, worry, sadness, or even panic, they do whatever they can to control it or get rid of it. Imagine you're applying for a job and the stress is really starting to get to you. You may start to worry that your résumé won't be good enough, or that the interviewer will think you sound stupid. The anxiety continues to build. To avoid feeling bad, you start to procrastinate on sending out job applications. Maybe you start mindlessly scrolling through social media posts, have a few glasses of wine, or avoid filling out the applications altogether. These behaviors may alleviate stress and anxiety in the

moment, but the relief is short-lived. These actions will only make bad feelings worse. Why? Because your behaviors are avoidant, meaning you are doing them to escape your feelings. Your avoidant behaviors are also in opposition to your goal (getting a job) and your values (such as being able to provide for your family). The further our behaviors take us from our values, the more at risk we are for developing increased stress, worry, and anxiety.

Think of your triggers as a garden, your emotions as flowers, and avoidance as water. The more you water the flowers, the bigger they get. And if you water your garden too often, it can become damaged and unable to grow flowers.

The Egg

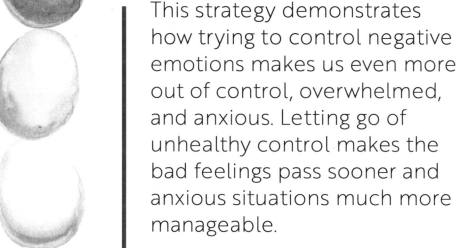

This strategy demonstrates how trying to control negative emotions makes us even more out of control, overwhelmed, and anxious. Letting go of unhealthy control makes the bad feelings pass sooner and anxious situations much more manageable.

What is your immediate, automatic answer to the following statement: "The best way to hold the egg so it doesn't break is..."

Imagine the following scenario:

You are given a raw egg that you must hold in your hand as you run up and down a set of stairs. It is your job to protect the egg from dropping and breaking.

RECORD THE RESPONSE THAT POPPED UP FOR YOU.

Most people's initial response is to hold the egg tightly to protect it from breaking. But what happens when we hold an egg tightly in our hand? That's right, it breaks. In your effort to keep the egg safe by holding it tighter, you create the exact outcome you tried so hard to prevent. This same idea holds true for a feeling. The more we try to control anxious worry, the worse it gets and the more helpless and out of control we feel.

WHAT, THEN, DO YOU THINK WOULD BE THE BEST WAY TO CARRY THE EGG SO THAT IT DOESN'T BREAK AS YOU RUN UP AND DOWN THE STAIRS?

The best way would probably be to put the egg in your hand and loosely cup your fingers around it.

In other words, less control = desired outcome.

CAN YOU THINK OF A SITUATION WHEN YOU TRIED TO CONTROL YOUR ANXIOUS SYMPTOMS (E.G., BY WORRYING) BUT ENDED UP FEELING EVEN MORE ANXIOUS AND OUT OF CONTROL?

HOW DID YOU TRY TO CONTROL YOUR ANXIETY? WHY DIDN'T YOUR EFFORTS WORK?

_____

_____

_____

_____

_____

_____

_____

_____

PROVIDE A FEW EXAMPLES OF ALTERNATIVE BEHAVIORS THAT MIGHT HAVE BEEN MORE EFFECTIVE.

1. _____

_____

_____

2. _____

_____

_____

3. _____

_____

_____

The Bathtub

Imagine you are about to go swimming. You step into the pool but immediately pull your foot out because the water feels way too cold. If you keep backing away when you try to go in, it will take much longer to get used to the water and, ultimately, take you longer to get in.

This exercise demonstrates the concept of sitting with discomfort. Feeling your feelings allows you to move forward. Struggling against your negative thoughts and feelings blocks you from moving forward, keeping you stuck in place.

_____

_____

_____

_____

_____

_____

_____

_____

_____

_____

_____

_____

_____

_____

_____

_____

_____

CHAPTER THREE

At first it may be uncomfortable, but keeping your foot in the water will allow you to get into the pool faster. The same idea applies to uncomfortable emotions. The more unwilling we are to sit with painful feelings, the longer we stay stuck in them.

Smile for the Camera

Choose a simple task or activity you can do for sixty seconds, such as tying your shoes, peeling a cucumber, or brushing your teeth. Record a video of you engaging in the task.

Differentiating between emotions, thoughts, physical sensations, and behaviors can be a tricky task for those who experience anxiety. It's not uncommon for people to label them incorrectly or neglect to see them as four distinct elements of anxiety. This exercise will teach you how to properly identify these four areas. It also demonstrates how it's still possible to perform a behavior regardless of your thoughts and feelings at the time.

When you are done, watch the video, then answer the
following questions:

1.	WHAT WAS I THINKING HERE?
2.	WHAT WAS I FEELING HERE?
3.	WHAT BODILY SENSATIONS WAS I EXPERIENCING HERE?
4.	WHAT AM I DOING IN THE VIDEO?

Next, show the video to someone else. Ask them the same questions and record their responses below:

1.	WHAT WAS I THINKING HERE?

2.	WHAT WAS I FEELING HERE?

3.	WHAT BODILY SENSATIONS WAS I EXPERIENCING HERE?

4.	WHAT AM I DOING IN THE VIDEO?

WHAT DO YOU NOTICE ABOUT THE OTHER PERSON'S RESPONSES?

NEXT, COMPARE THEIR RESPONSES TO YOUR OWN. WHAT DO YOU NOTICE?

OF THE FOUR COMPONENTS OF ANXIETY, WHICH ONES ARE DIRECTLY OBSERVABLE IN THE VIDEO? WHICH ONES ARE NOT?

WHAT, THEN, DOES THIS TELL YOU ABOUT THE RELATIONSHIP BETWEEN OUR EMOTIONS, THOUGHTS, PHYSICAL SENSATIONS, AND BEHAVIORS?

You Do You

Write down five things you value most in life. Next, record one behavior that aligns with that value. For example, if you value being a good friend, you may make extra efforts to check in with those who you know are struggling. Think of your values as a destination and your goals as little things you need to accomplish along your journey.

For each day, try to intentionally engage in at least one behavior that aligns with the values you listed above. Record how you felt before, during, and after doing the behavior.

We all get caught up in the stress of our day-to-day. Despite our fast-paced lives, it is important to fill our days with the things we value most in life. The less of a match there is between our day-to-day behaviors and our values, the more at risk we become for developing anxiety disorders and having an overall decrease in mental well-being. This exercise, adapted from Steven Hayes's work on value-driven behavior, will help you to identify your own values.

M-F	VALUE	BEHAVIOR
M	1.	
T		
W		
TH		
F		
M	2.	
T		
W		
TH		
F		
M	3.	
T		
W		
TH		
F		
M	4.	
T		
W		
TH		
F		
M	5.	
T		
W		
TH		
F		

	SUNDAY	MONDAY	TUESDAY
Intentional behavior			
What value this behavior aligns with			
How I felt before the behavior			
How I felt while I was doing the behavior			
How I felt after completing the behavior			

CHAPTER THREE

Sink or Swim

Think of some instances when you used a particular strategy or behavior to avoid feeling anxious, then answer the questions that follow.

Sometimes value-based behaviors make us uncomfortable. Let's say you value being a good student, yet you frequently procrastinate when you become overwhelmed with schoolwork. Your procrastination helps you avoid feeling the stress of your work. It may make you feel better in the moment, but the relief is only temporary, as your anxiety will intensify later when you miss your deadline.

However, by sticking to a reasonable schedule, despite feeling stressed, you will ensure you meet your deadline with way less anxiety than if you had procrastinated. The goal is to sit with your discomfort and at the same time do the behavior (keep to your schedule) that moves you closer to your value (being a good student).

STRATEGY USED TO AVOID YOUR ANXIETY/STRESS

DID IT WORK AT FIRST?

DID IT KEEP YOUR ANXIETY FROM COMING BACK LATER?

IF NOT, DID IT FEEL WORSE, BETTER, OR THE SAME?

DID THE BEHAVIOR HELP YOU MOVE TOWARD YOUR VALUES OR AWAY FROM THEM?

_____

_____

_____

_____

_____

IS THERE A BETTER WAY YOU COULD HAVE HANDLED THIS SITUATION?

_____

_____

_____

_____

_____

_____

_____

_____

_____

_____

_____

_____

_____

_____

Strategy of Struggling

Over the next few days, record some instances in which you feel stuck.

Emotions are a normal part of everyday life. They come up, they shift, they get worse, they improve, they leave, and then the cycle starts again. As we know, not all emotions are fun to have. In fact, some can feel uncomfortable and even scary. It makes sense that we try so hard to block these uncomfortable feelings. Unfortunately, avoiding them creates a never-ending struggle between our ourselves and our thoughts and feelings.

Our thoughts multiply into worry, we try to argue them away, and we choose behaviors opposed to our values, all just to avoid feeling bad. This strategy of struggling against our bad thoughts and feelings doesn't work; it keeps us stuck in a toxic cycle of avoidance and anxiety.

BRIEFLY DESCRIBE THE TRIGGER OR SITUATION.

_____

_____

_____

_____

_____

_____

WHAT WAS YOUR VERY FIRST FEELING AND/OR THOUGHT?

_____

_____

_____

_____

WHAT LEVEL (MILD, MODERATE, STRONG) WOULD YOU RATE YOUR DISCOMFORT?

_____

_____

_____

_____

WHAT DID YOUR INTERNAL STRUGGLE LOOK LIKE (E.G., YELLING, DRINKING, TRYING TO FORGET HOW YOU FEEL, JUDGING YOURSELF)?

_____

_____

_____

_____

_____

_____

_____

_____

_____

WHAT IMPACT DID YOUR STRUGGLE HAVE ON YOUR INITIAL DISCOMFORT? DID IT BECOME BETTER, WORSE, OR STAY THE SAME?

_____

_____

_____

_____

_____

_____

_____

_____

_____

Briefly describe the trigger or situation.

What was your very first feeling and/or thought?

What level (mild, moderate, strong) would you rate your discomfort?

What did your internal struggle look like (e.g., yelling, drinking, trying to forget how you feel, judging yourself)?

What impact did your struggle have on your initial discomfort? Did it become better, worse, or stay the same?

Briefly describe the trigger or situation.

What was your very first feeling and/or thought?

What level (mild, moderate, strong) would you rate your discomfort?

What did your internal struggle look like (e.g., yelling, drinking, trying to forget how you feel, judging yourself)?

What impact did your struggle have on your initial discomfort? Did it become better, worse, or stay the same?

TUESDAY

Briefly describe the trigger or situation.

What was your very first feeling and/or thought?

What level (mild, moderate, strong) would you rate your discomfort?

What did your internal struggle look like (e.g., yelling, drinking, trying to forget how you feel, judging yourself)?

What impact did your struggle have on your initial discomfort? Did it become better, worse, or stay the same?

THURSDAY

Briefly describe the trigger or situation.

What was your very first feeling and/or thought?

What level (mild, moderate, strong) would you rate your discomfort?

What did your internal struggle look like (e.g., yelling, drinking, trying to forget how you feel, judging yourself)?

What impact did your struggle have on your initial discomfort? Did it become better, worse, or stay the same?

SATURDAY

Busy Bee

Read the following scenario and answer the questions that follow:

This exercise, adapted from Dr. Steven Hayes's exercise "Passengers on the Bus," will help you formulate better solutions in the moment when a bad feeling escalates and you feel the urge to get rid of it. It is a useful skill to have in your toolbox to keep you from becoming stuck, especially when you encounter a difficult situation (e.g., you become frustrated because your boss asked you to work on a weekend).

You are invited to a picnic at the lake with your friends. As you walk alongside the lake to meet them, you hear a loud humming. You turn toward the noise and see a massive swarm of mosquitos by the lake. At first you freeze, unsure about what to do, but then decide to keep going. As you start walking, though, the swarm chases after you. You immediately stop and stand perfectly still. And when you do, the swarm flies back to their lake spot, leaving you alone.

WHAT DO YOU DO?

Now let's imagine that each mosquito represents a negative thought or feeling. If you stay put, these thoughts and feelings will leave you alone. If you continue to walk toward the picnic area, they will swarm you. There is good news, though! You remembered to wear bug spray! So, while these difficult feelings may swarm you, they can't touch you.

WOULD THIS KNOWLEDGE CHANGE THE STRATEGY YOU LISTED ABOVE? AND IF SO, HOW?

It may feel more comfortable to stay put since the mosquitos leave you alone. You could also just go home. Cancelling plans certainly takes the fear and worry away—temporarily.

> **WHAT, IF ANY, ARE THE DISADVANTAGES OF THESE TWO STRATEGIES? WOULD THEY BE CONSISTENT WITH YOUR VALUES?**

To Do or Not to Do

Follow these instructions, then answer the questions:

1. Tell yourself "I must jump up and down," and while you say this, stand in place with both feet on the floor.

2. Say to yourself "I can't open my eyes," yet keep your eyes wide open.

3. Tell yourself "I have purple-and-green striped hair," then go look in a mirror.

This strategy highlights the power of behaviors. People with anxiety frequently make assumptions that they can't do something because they feel a certain way. For example, "I can't speak in public because it's too scary" or "There is no way I can go on a date with him; just look at me!" While anxious thoughts and feelings may have some influence on our behaviors, they do not control or cause them.

DID YOU JUMP UP AND DOWN?

WERE YOU UNABLE TO OPEN YOUR EYES?

WAS YOUR HAIR PURPLE AND GREEN?

WHAT DOES THIS DEMONSTRATE?

THINK OF A TIME WHEN YOU ASSUMED THAT YOUR THOUGHTS AND/OR EMOTIONS CAUSED A BEHAVIOR, THEN ANSWER THE FOLLOW-UP ITEMS BELOW. WHAT WERE THE THOUGHTS/EMOTIONS? WHAT WAS THE BEHAVIOR(S)?

DID YOUR BEHAVIOR IN THIS SITUATION TAKE YOU CLOSER TO YOUR VALUES?

DID THIS BEHAVIOR MAKE YOU LESS ANXIOUS IN THE MOMENT?

DID THIS BEHAVIOR INCREASE YOUR ANXIETY LATER? WHY?

Liar, Liar, Mind on Fire

Provide three examples of anxious thoughts that lied to you about your ability to do something.

Just like thoughts don't control our behaviors, they also don't speak the truth. Yes, our anxious thoughts lie to us. A lot. How many times have you said to yourself something like "I can't go to the party. I'm way too anxious"? Does anxiety truly make you physically incapable of going to the party? No. You can feel anxious and still attend.

1. _____

_____

_____

_____

2. _____

_____

_____

_____

3. _____

_____

_____

_____

Anxious thoughts are excuses we use to get out of doing something uncomfortable. They are often fear based and inaccurate. Using the previous party scenario, genuine "realistic explanations" why you can't attend may include any of the following:

❖ You are sick with fever
❖ You have a work deadline to meet
❖ It's the same weekend as a good friend's wedding

Look back at the anxious thoughts you listed above. For each, list a realistic explanation for why you could or couldn't do something.

1. _____

_____

_____

_____

_____

_____

_____

_____

_____

_____

_____

_____

_____

_____

_____

_____

_____

_____

_____

2. _____

_____

_____

_____

_____

_____

_____

_____

_____

_____

3. _____

_____

_____

_____

_____

_____

_____

Becoming aware of your false thinking and distinguishing fact from fiction are effective strategies that promote healthy behaviors and help you to effectively manage daily stress and anxiety.

Fraudulent Feelings

Emotions, like thoughts, do not cause behaviors. This exercise will help you become more aware of your behaviors in the moment to ensure that your emotions do not dictate your actions. When we use emotions as our reasons for not doing something, we incorrectly assume that our feelings have control over our behaviors, rather than ourselves. This suggests that we can't change our behaviors unless we change our feelings first, when in fact, our behaviors can be changed regardless of our mood.

PICK SOMETHING THAT CAUSES YOU CONSIDERABLE STRESS AND ANXIETY.

_____

_____

_____

_____

For 60 seconds, sit with whatever you listed. Notice the anxiety it brings up for you. Pay attention to your body, including heart rate, tension, and so on. Now, pick a simple behavior (e.g., getting the mail). Say to yourself: "I can't [get the mail] because I feel anxious." Continue to repeat this statement while, at the same exact time, doing the behavior you listed above.

DID YOUR ANXIOUS FEELING PREVENT YOU FROM DOING THE BEHAVIOR YOU LISTED?

_____

_____

WHY NOT? WAS IT DIFFICULT?

_____

_____

_____

_____

_____

_____

_____

CHAPTER THREE

WHAT ARE SOME POSSIBLE CONSEQUENCES HAD YOU NOT DONE THE BEHAVIOR (E.G., IF I DIDN'T GET THE MAIL BECAUSE I WAS TOO ANXIOUS, I PROBABLY WOULDN'T HAVE BEEN ABLE TO TAKE THE TRASH OUT TONIGHT EITHER).

_____

_____

_____

_____

_____

_____

_____

WHAT DID YOU NOTICE ABOUT YOUR EMOTIONS AFTER DOING THE BEHAVIOR/ NOT DOING THE BEHAVIOR?

_____

_____

_____

_____

_____

_____

_____

_____

_____

LOOK AT THE BEHAVIORS YOU LISTED. DO YOU SEE A COMMON THEME?
IS THERE A SPECIFIC PATTERN TO THEM?

_____

_____

_____

_____

_____

_____

_____

_____

WHAT DID YOU FIND DIFFICULT ABOUT THIS EXERCISE?

_____

_____

_____

_____

_____

_____

_____

_____

CHAPTER THREE

	SUNDAY	MONDAY	TUESDAY
Behavior:			
Emotion:			
Rate strength of emotion from 1 to 10:			
Did you do the behavior? (y/n):			
Emotion rating after doing/ not doing behavior:			

CHAPTER THREE

Opposites Do Not Attract

When our behaviors are emotion-driven, we are more likely to do something impulsive and unhealthy. These types of behaviors often have unfavorable outcomes, further fueling bad feelings and thoughts. For example, say you are having a horrible day at work. You're angry and agitated. Even though you have a big meeting the next morning, you go out drinking anyway. You miss your meeting because you drank too much and slept through your alarm. Your anger and agitation from the day before is not only worse, but now you're also extremely anxious that you will get fired.

An effective way to ensure behaviors are not heavily influenced by mood is to do the exact opposite of what our urges and emotions are telling us. This is why being in the present moment is key to anxiety management. The more present we are, the easier it is to pause, consider our response options, and choose a healthy behavior.

Below is a list of behaviors that are likely to have negative consequences. For each behavior, provide an opposite response:

1. Going drinking after a horrible day at work with a meeting early the next morning.

2. Getting in the car to drive around after an explosive argument with your significant other.

3. Being so anxious about your end-of-year project that you completely avoid doing it.

Respond to the following questions based on a recent time your behavior was driven by anxious emotions, resulting in a negative outcome.

BRIEFLY DESCRIBE THE SITUATION THAT TRIGGERED YOUR ANXIETY.

WHAT EMOTION WERE YOU EXPERIENCING AT THAT TIME?

WHAT BEHAVIOR DID YOU ENGAGE IN BASED ON YOUR NEGATIVE MOOD?

_____

_____

_____

_____

_____

WHAT WAS THE OUTCOME OF THIS BEHAVIOR?

_____

_____

_____

_____

_____

PROVIDE AN EXAMPLE OF A BEHAVIOR THAT WOULD BE THE OPPOSITE OF YOUR RESPONSE.

_____

_____

_____

_____

_____

_____

HAD YOU DONE THE OPPOSITE BEHAVIOR YOU LISTED ABOVE, DO YOU THINK
YOUR ANXIETY WOULD HAVE BEEN WORSE WHILE DOING IT? WHY OR WHY NOT?

_____

_____

_____

_____

_____

_____

_____

_____

WHAT MIGHT HAVE BEEN THE OUTCOME HAD YOU DONE THE
OPPOSITE BEHAVIOR?

_____

_____

_____

_____

_____

_____

_____

_____

_____

_____

An Apple a Day

Keeps Your Stress Right in Front of You

Imagine you are picking apples to make a pie. You choose to use a large sack, rather than a big clunky cart, to collect your apples. Each apple represents a life stressor (e.g., finances, work, marriage, kids, health, the tennis match you have next week). What would your apples represent?

Life is not without stress and anxiety. A fulfilled life still includes stress and anxiety, but we are able to carry it in a nontoxic way (without trying to control it or push it away). This strategy demonstrates how holding our anxiety differently leads to healthy and valued behavior change.

_____

_____

_____

_____

When your sack becomes filled, you decided to head home. The bag is way too heavy to carry, so you drag it behind you on the walk to your car. Eager to get home, you continue to lug the apples up the hill to your car. It doesn't take long before your arms start aching. These apples are weighing you down. You're sweating, struggling, and making very little progress. At the same time, you won't leave the apples because you spent hours picking them. You also need them for baking. What can you do?

_____

_____

_____

_____

_____

_____

YOU SUDDENLY REMEMBER THAT BIG, CLUNKY PUSHCART FROM EARLIER AND GO BACK TO GET IT. HOW WOULD THIS HELP YOUR SITUATION?

_____

_____

_____

_____

_____

_____

_____

Now try to apply this scenario to your own life. Record your responses to the questions below.

HOW DOES SHIFTING THE WAY YOU CARRY A PARTICULAR STRESSOR IMPACT YOUR DAILY LIFE?

WHAT WOULD THIS SHIFT LOOK LIKE?

DOES SHIFTING HELP REALIGN YOUR BEHAVIORS WITH YOUR VALUES? WHY?

WHAT WOULD YOU CHOOSE TO DO WITH ALL THE TIME NO LONGER SPENT ON
STRUGGLING WITH YOUR STRESSOR?

Places, People, & Patterns.

Everyone can think of a time when they overreacted in a situation, only to realize later that their behaviors were out of line. Maybe you uncharacteristically snapped at your child because they left their jacket in the middle of the floor. You honked your horn a bit too loud and a little too long at the driver in front of you who didn't immediately go when the light turned green. Or you got a flat tire when you were already 30 minutes late for work, so you threw your phone across the highway out of anger.

What makes us respond in ways that are out of proportion to what happened? In other words, why are our responses sometimes way bigger than the situation itself? Most of the time, it's because you're not actually responding to the situation in the present, but rather to something that occurred in the past. This exercise will help you to identify situations that may trigger a big response and give you the tools to modify your behavior in the moment.

Think of a time when your response to something was above and beyond what the situation called for.

WHERE DID THIS OCCUR (E.G., AT THE MARKET)?

WHO ELSE WAS INVOLVED (E.G., ANOTHER WOMAN IN LINE AT THE STORE)?

WHAT WAS YOUR BEHAVIORAL RESPONSE (E.G., ABRUPTLY LEFT STORE)?

WHAT WAS YOUR COGNITIVE RESPONSE (E.G., "HOW DARE THEY SPEAK TO ME LIKE THAT!")?

_____

_____

_____

_____

_____

_____

_____

WHAT WAS YOUR EMOTIONAL RESPONSE (E.G., ANGER, SADNESS)?

_____

_____

_____

_____

_____

_____

_____

DID SOMETHING HAPPEN BEFORE THIS EVENT THAT MAY HAVE HEIGHTENED YOUR RESPONSE?

_____

_____

_____

_____

_____

_____

_____

_____

DID ANYTHING IN THIS SITUATION REMIND YOU OF SOMEONE FROM YOUR PAST
(E.G., WOMAN AT THE MARKET LOOKED LIKE YOUR SISTER; IT'S THE SAME STORE
YOUR FATHER WORKED AT)?

DID THIS SITUATION REMIND YOU OF A TIME WHEN YOU FELT A SIMILAR WAY?

Situation	
Behavioral response	
Emotion	
Thoughts	
Any memories triggered in the moment?	
Any familiar feelings or thoughts?	

AT THE END OF THE WEEK, GO BACK AND REVIEW YOUR CHART. DO YOU NOTICE ANY PATTERNS IN YOUR BEHAVIORS?

DO YOU NOTICE ANY THEMES ACROSS YOUR THINKING?

2.   3.

HOW ABOUT WITH YOUR FEELINGS?

_____

_____

_____

WHERE DO YOU THINK THESE PATTERNS COME FROM?

_____

_____

_____

Anticipation Station

This exercise focuses on a concept known as "anticipatory anxiety," or the anxiety you think you will have while doing something that makes you extremely uncomfortable. In other words, it's anxiety about having anxiety. For example, your course syllabus says that on July 11, you must present a research project to the class worth 50 percent of your final grade. Your anxiety skyrockets and you're now consumed by worry. All you can think about is being judged by your classmates, having a panic attack in front of everyone, and being viewed as stupid by your professor. The anxiety leading up to July 11 is almost unbearable. This is anticipatory anxiety. There is, however, good news! Anticipatory anxiety is almost always worse than the anxiety you will actually have in the situation.

- ❖ Future-oriented triggering event (e.g., pending doctor appointment, hosting a dinner party later that week)
- ❖ Rate your level of anxiety (0 to 100) in the days leading up to the event
- ❖ Rate your level of anxiety (0 to 100) during the actual event
- ❖ Rate your level of anxiety (0 to 100) after the event is over

THE EVENT	UP-TO (0-100)	DURING (0-100)	AFTER (0-100)

WHAT WAS YOUR EXPERIENCE WHILE DOING THIS EXERCISE? WAS IT DIFFICULT FOR YOU? IF SO, WHY?

WHAT DID YOU NOTICE ABOUT YOUR ANTICIPATORY ANXIETY?

DESCRIBE ANY DIFFERENCES YOU NOTICED BETWEEN YOUR ANXIETY DURING AND AFTER THE EVENT.

_____

_____

_____

_____

_____

_____

_____

WHAT DO YOU THINK WOULD HAVE HAPPENED IF YOU HAD AVOIDED THE SITUATION ALTOGETHER?

_____

_____

_____

_____

_____

_____

_____

_____

_____

Slow and Steady Wins the Race

People put a ton of mental energy and effort into avoiding the things that make them feel bad, especially the things that make them anxious. As we know, when we avoid the things that make us anxious, three things happen. First, we send the message to ourselves that we are incapable of doing the task we are avoiding. Second, we continue to confirm to ourselves that we are powerless against our anxiety. Lastly, we make our anxiety symptoms worse, creating a vicious cycle of anxiety and avoidance.

A technique known as graded exposure moves us toward our anxious discomfort, rather than away from it, in a very systematic approach. The goal of graded exposure is to slowly break through the avoidance of anxiety-producing situations and increase our tolerance of anxious thoughts, feelings, and sensations. What may seem like an easy task to others may feel like climbing a mountain to those with anxiety; it's just too overwhelming and could set you up for failure. It is important to break apart the situations into what I like to call "insultingly small tasks." These small, manageable, and achievable goals can give you a sense of mastery and hope.

Think of a situation you often avoid because it makes you incredibly anxious, overwhelmed, or stressed (e.g., cleaning your house).

_____

_____

Break down the situation you listed above into ten separate steps. For example, cleaning your house can be broken down into putting away laundry, washing dishes, wiping the countertops down in the kitchen, and so on.

1. _____
2. _____
3. _____
4. _____
5. _____
6. _____
7. _____
8. _____
9. _____
10. _____

On a scale of 1 to 10 (1 being least anxiety-producing and 10 being most), rate the items on your list without using the same number twice. Put the rating next to each item.

NEXT, REWRITE YOUR TEN STEPS IN THE ORDER YOU RANKED THEM, BEGINNING WITH THE LEAST ANXIETY-INDUCING.

_____

_____

_____

_____

_____

THE EVENT	RATING BEFORE	RATING DURING	RATING AFTER
1.			
2.			
3.			
4.			
5.			
6.			
7.			
8.			
9.			
10.			

Now, try doing these tasks in order daily. It is important not to rush through the items. If you "grin and bear it," you are preventing yourself from fully experiencing your anxiety in the moment. Only once you have minimal to no anxiety should you move onto the next task.

As you tackle each step, be sure to keep a record of how and what you are feeling. Use the spaces on the next page to journal your experiences as you master this. Using the tracking chart above, you will also rate your anxiety level before, during and after the completion using a scale of 1 to 100.

Once you have completed your entire list, answer the following questions:

WHAT DID YOU NOTICE ABOUT YOUR ANXIETY AS YOU WORKED YOUR WAY
THROUGH THE LIST?

_____

_____

_____

_____

_____

WHAT OBSTACLES DID YOU ENCOUNTER? HOW DID YOU OVERCOME THEM?

_____

_____

_____

_____

HAD YOU ATTEMPTED TO MASTER THIS ALL AT ONCE, WHAT DO YOU BELIEVE THE
OUTCOME WOULD HAVE BEEN AND HOW WOULD IT HAVE IMPACTED
YOUR ANXIETY?

_____

_____

_____

_____

_____

_____

It's Time to Make Time

The amount of time we spend struggling against the things we don't want to think and feel can be substantial. The battle sucks us right out of the moment and locks us up in our minds, resulting in a worsening of stress, anxiety, and even depression. It hinders our ability to be present and lead a fulfilled life doing the things we enjoy and find meaningful.

LIST THE STRUGGLES YOU FIND MOST CONSUMING AND OVERWHELMING.	APPROXIMATE AMOUNT OF **TIME PER DAY** YOU SPEND ON THESE STRUGGLES.
1.	
2.	
3.	
4.	
5.	
6.	
7.	
8.	
9.	
10.	

Once your chart is complete, answer the following questions:

1. Approximately what amount of time total per day do you spend struggling against unwanted thoughts and feelings?

2. If you reduce this amount of time by half, how much time do you free up?

3. What would you do with all this free time if you weren't stuck struggling in your head? Make a list of five to ten enjoyable, value-based behaviors you could choose from.

1. _____

_____

_____

_____

2. _____

_____

_____

_____

3. _____

_____

_____

4. _____

_____

_____

_____

5.

6.

7.

8.

9.

10.

CHAPTER THREE

Conclusion

It is my hope that this workbook has given you a comprehensive understanding of anxiety and that it has also equipped you with the tools to successfully manage it along with everyday stress. Many of us have been stuck in unhealthy patterns for decades. As we get older and life circumstances change, our patterns of behavior should adjust accordingly. Some patterns need only a slight modification, while others need a complete overhaul. Some remain highly effective, while others have become detrimental. While at one point in our lives, these patterns may have well been adaptive, they are now toxic and are the very things that are keeping us stuck. It is the goal of this workbook to help the reader untangle themselves from the clutter and chaos that live in their mind.

Progress is a journey, not a destination, and it's important to set accurate expectations of your anxiety along the way. Remember, we can't fully eliminate our anxiety, because it is a necessary and naturally occurring emotion. It gives us information about our surroundings and informs us of danger. Without it, we would have no warning system to alert us to potentially harmful threats. Racing heart, shortness of breath, and increased tightness in our muscles are all adaptive responses—but only when a real threat is present. When these symptoms occur in the absence of danger and we struggle to shut them off, they heighten in intensity. While these sensations may feel bad, even unbearable at times, trying to avoid, suppress, or control them makes them stick around even longer. Therefore, it's so important to develop tools to sit with this

discomfort, to essentially do nothing with it, and allow it to pass. Like an ocean wave, feelings rise, peak, and then come down on their own. If we continue to struggle against the wave, we will exhaust ourselves and get knocked down. In both situations, the wave still rises, peaks, and comes down. Either way, it's happening. The real question is, Do you want to exhaust yourself in the struggle against the wave? Or do you want to stand next to it, watching it fall, while you conserve your energy for things you value?

The struggle we get into with our icky feelings can look very different for each of us. For some, it's social isolation, perfectionism, or worry. For others, it may be drinking, drug use, or gambling. All of these behaviors take us away from our values, negatively impacting our mental health. This is why identifying these avoidant behaviors is a core component of this workbook. Increasing our awareness in the present moment helps us target, then change, our unhelpful behaviors. Using the exercises to guide you, you can choose healthier, value-consistent behaviors to promote a more fulfilled, purposeful life.

Anxiety and everyday stress can be overwhelming and, at times, paralyzing. But they are very treatable. Development of awareness, tolerance of discomfort, and identifying healthy, value-driven behaviors will take you out of the struggle and shift you into the present moment. Remember, this is a process, and rarely is it an easy one. It takes time, willingness, and patience, so be gentle with yourself.

ABOUT THE WORKBOOK

The exercises in this workbook are adaptations from various therapies, all of which are evidence-based practices. Acceptance and commitment therapy (ACT), mindfulness-based cognitive therapy (MBCT), dialectical behavior therapy (DBT), and cognitive behavioral therapy (CBT) have repeatedly been found effective in treating several psychological disorders, including major depression, generalized anxiety disorder, panic disorder, social anxiety disorder, post-traumatic stress disorder, and obsessive-compulsive disorder.

Over the last twenty years, I have used a combination of these therapies in my clinical practice. Just as the strategies are presented to you in this workbook, I pull exercises and tools from these various approaches based on my patients' needs, interaction styles, and diagnoses. The strategies I use, both with my patients and in this workbook, are couched in behavior therapy, meaning there is a large emphasis placed on the importance of changing and modifying unhelpful patterns of behavior.

I would like to acknowledge the essential groundbreaking work of Drs. Steven Hayes, Kelly Wilson, Aaron Beck, Zindel Segal, Mark Williams, John Teasdale, and Marsha Linehan. Their theories are the framework behind many of the exercises presented in this workbook.

ACKNOWLEDGMENTS

First and foremost, I would like to thank Quarto Publishing for presenting me with the opportunity to write this workbook. Thank you to Katie Moore for your patience, insight, and edits throughout this entire writing process.

To my colleagues, Drs. Jen Wolkin and Rachel Goldman, and Ann-Louise T. Lockhart, thank you for always sharing your wisdom, support, and unique friendship. Special thank you to Dr. Terri Bacow for tirelessly answering all my questions. I am greatly appreciative of the amazing Instagram community of mental health professionals I have come to know and whose work and knowledge has truly been invaluable. Thank you to Tesia and John Barone, the creative geniuses responsible for the development of my website and the artistic design of my social media pages.

Many thanks to all my professors, clinical supervisors, and mentors over the years who have guided me through graduate school and beyond and whose influence remains an integral part of my clinical practice today. I would like to acknowledge the essential groundbreaking work of Drs. Steven Hayes, Kelly Wilson, Aaron Beck, Zindel Segal, Mark Williams, John Teasdale, and Marsha Linehan. Their theories are the framework behind many of the exercises presented in this workbook.

To my "people," my childhood and college friends, "mom" friends, tennis crew, and work buddies, you have been an integral part of my career journey and your friendships are invaluable. To Donna and Caroline, to say my family would be lost without you is an understatement. Thank you both for just being you. And lastly, to my family, thank you for your never-ending support, understanding, and patience throughout this entire process. None of this would have been possible without you.

ABOUT THE AUTHOR

Dr. Jaime Zuckerman is a graduate of the Ohio State University and obtained her doctorate in clinical psychology from La Salle University. She trained at various Philadelphia-area hospitals, including Temple University and the University of Pennsylvania's prestigious Center for Cognitive Therapy. She completed both her predoctoral internship and postdoctoral training at Long Island Jewish Medical Center in Queens, New York.

Dr. Z is a licensed clinical psychologist in private practice outside Philadelphia, focusing on both Cognitive Behavioral Therapy and Acceptance and Commitment Therapy in her treatment of adults. She specializes in anxiety disorders, depression, and adjustment to medical illness. Dr. Z's clinical work also focuses on assisting those in relationships with narcissistic partners and helping them heal from narcissistic abuse.

Dr. Z is a mental health social media influencer in addition to being a media contributor. She has been featured in publications including Vogue, Shape, the Harvard Business Review, Women's Health, and the Washington Post, with an Ask the Expert column in Verywell Health. Dr. Z is an on-air mental health expert guest on various podcasts and news outlets, including Fox29 News, PHL 17, CBS3 Philly, Daily Mail TV, and The List TV.

She is cohost of It's Me, Dr. Z with JB, a weekly podcast that dives into various mental health topics from the standpoint of both psychologist and patient. Dr. Z is also a board member of the Epilepsy Foundation of Eastern Pennsylvania (EFEPA) and is a frequent conference presenter for both the EFEPA and the Dravet Syndrome Foundation.

Dr. Z lives in the suburbs of Philadelphia with her husband and three children. When not working/reading/writing/speaking/posting and momming, she loves playing tennis, reading psychological thrillers, and watching good documentaries.

For additional mental health resources, including virtual workshops, social media, videos, article features, and TV appearance links, please see the links below.

Website: www.drjaimezuckerman.com
Podcast: It's Me, Dr. Z with JB, available on Apple Podcasts or wherever you listen to your podcasts
Instagram: @dr.z_psychologist
Twitter: @drzpsychologist
YouTube: Dr. Jaime Zuckerman
Facebook: @drjaimespinellzuckerman